If I Were A...
TEACHER
The world of teaching in pictures!

NorthParadePublishing

Published in 2010 by North Parade Publishing Ltd.
4 North Parade
Bath
BA1 1LF
UK

© North Parade Publishing Ltd.

If I Were A...
TEACHER
The world of teaching in pictures!

INTRODUCTION

Right from the age of 4 or 5 when most children start going to school, teachers have a great degree of influence on their development. This is an influence that the teacher continues to play throughout the formative years of the child's life.

This book is a pictorial journey through the world of the teacher.

An easy read book, it acquaints children with the various activities that a teacher performs.

The pictures in the book have been carefully selected to illustrate the teacher's role and the brief, bite-sized text provide informative captions.

Teachers work with children in schools. They tell the children about the important things in life, so they can grow up to be good people and live a good life.

Teachers have to be really creative. They have to constantly come up with new games and activities to make learning fun for children.

Children learn by doing. The job of the teacher is to help children explore and discover the world for themselves.

A good teacher will involve themselves in the children's activities. They will do the activities with the children while teaching them at the same time.

A teacher should always encourage the students. They should not say anything negative about any student. Their job is to tell the student what they did right, not what they did wrong.

It is not easy to be a teacher.
There are often many children in
a class who must all be looked
after equally.

New Words
angel   sleigh
automobile   stagecoach
buggy   swayback
carriage   transportatio
dream   visio
horse   wag

Teaching is not just
about taking tests
and giving out grades.
Teachers have to gain
the trust of the children,
so the students can be
comfortable with them.

Children are like cats, naturally curious. The teacher has to help the students in finding answers and satisfying that curiosity.

A teacher needs to have a lot of patience. Children will often ask the same things in many different ways. The teacher needs to give the same answer in new ways.

When a teacher participates in the learning activities along with the children, they are telling the child that it is something important and worth learning.

When a teacher provides children with an environment where they are free to play, they help them to develop their skills.

In order to ensure that the child develops well, the teacher needs to begin by observing the children at play.

Then the teacher makes adjustments to the space, materials and the rules for play so the children are able to enjoy more and learn more.

Teachers who encourage and accept students' questions and comments without judgement and explain ideas by breaking them down into simpler terms stimulate the exchange of ideas.

The teacher is there to guide each child through every step in the process of discovery. Children need reassurance that they are doing things correctly and well.

It might be difficult to watch over every child. But, the teacher has to be careful that no child feels neglected. Some children will need more attention than others.

Children are often scared to do things for the first time. Teachers need to encourage these activities too. With their help and support they'll grow more confident.

The teacher has to make every student feel like an individual while thinking of the benefit of the whole class at the same time.

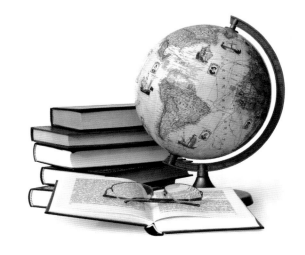

A teacher has to find new and innovative ways to beat the monotony of classroom teaching. A change in environment can be exciting.

To ensure all-round development of the children, they have to be taught new and challenging skills.

Children will often trust their teacher implicitly. The teacher's words and actions are important to them.

The teacher must not do anything to shake the children's trust in them.

On the chalkboard:

$1 \times 4 = 4$
$2 \times 4 = 8$
$3 \times 4 = 12$
$4 \times 4 = 16$
$4 \times 5 = 20$
$4 \times 6 = 24$
$4 \times 7 = 28$

A teacher has to make each and every one of their students feel special. A smile or an encouraging word can do wonders for children.

Children love to be in a group. A teacher has to be a part of that group. The children must think of her as one of their own.

When they are learning, the first few steps are the most important for children. Teachers have to navigate the children through all the set-backs carefully.

Sometimes, the teacher needs to keep a watchful eye from afar. Children need to make their own mistakes and learn to pick themselves up after they fall.

When correcting a child's mistake, the teacher has to be very careful. Mistakes don't lead to failures, harsh criticism does.

The smallest
achievements of the
children have to be
celebrated by the
teacher. Every child
needs to feel special.

Children need to know
they can accomplish
anything and everything.
The teacher has to do
everything to make them
believe in themselves.

The teacher also needs to enjoy their activities if they want the children to enjoy them. Children won't have fun if their teacher isn't having fun.

GLOSSARY

Accomplish: to complete or finish a task or activity or achieve a goal

Confident: sure of oneself and one's abilities

Creative: someone with the power or ability to create something new

Criticism: giving a negative opinion on something

Curious: eager to learn or know something

Discover: to see, get knowledge of, or find out for oneself

Encourage: inspiring someone to do better

Environment: the conditions or things around someone or in a place

Explore: find out for oneself

Failure: not achieving the desired result

Hurdles:	difficult problems to be overcome
Inferior:	less important or worthy
Innovative:	see creative
Navigate:	to direct or manage
Neglect:	pay no attention to
Patient:	willing to wait for results
Reassure:	assure again to boost someone's confidence
Skill:	the ability to do something well
Stimulate:	excite or rouse someone to action
Teacher:	a person who teaches or instructs
Trust:	rely on